Wrestling Superstars

Rhea Ripley

By Kaitlyn Duling

Torque

Torque, an imprint of Bellwether Media by Flutterbee

Torque brims with excitement perfect for thrill-seekers of all kinds. Discover daring survival skills, explore uncharted worlds, and marvel at mighty engines and extreme sports. In *Torque* books, anything can happen. Are you ready?

This edition first published in 2027 by Bellwether Media, Inc.

For information regarding permission, write to Bellwether Media, Inc., Attention: Permissions Department, 3500 American Blvd W, Suite 150, Bloomington, MN 55431.

Library of Congress Cataloging-in-Publication Data is available at www.loc.gov or upon request from the publisher.

ISBN: 9798898801106 (hardcover)
ISBN: 9798898802349 (ebook)

Editor: Suzane Nguyen   Series Designer: Gabriel Hilger

Printed in the United States of America, North Mankato, MN.

TABLE OF CONTENTS

MAKING HISTORY

Wrestlemania 39 has been a tough battle. It is the final **match** between Rhea Ripley and Charlotte Flair. Ripley and Flair fight on the ropes. But Ripley knocks Flair out!

Ripley climbs onto the ropes. She picks Flair up. Wham! Ripley slams Flair onto the mat. The crowd cheers! Ripley is now the SmackDown Women's Champion!

WHO IS RHEA RIPLEY?

INKED!

Ripley has more than a dozen tattoos. Each one holds a different meaning for her.

Rhea Ripley is a **World Wrestling Entertainment (WWE)** superstar! She is the first female Australian champion in WWE history. She has been in WWE since 2017. Ripley won six **titles** in her first eight years with WWE.

RHEA RIPLEY

BIRTHDAY
OCTOBER 11, 1996

HOMETOWN
ADELAIDE, AUSTRALIA

COMPANY
WWE

HEIGHT
5'7"

THEME SONG

"Demon in Your Dreams"
def Rebel, Motionless in White

Fans love Ripley's tattoos, dark makeup, and edgy style. They root for her to win even though she is a **heel**.

GROWING UP DOWN UNDER

Rhea Ripley grew up in Adelaide, Australia. As a child, she was very active.

She played many sports, including rugby, karate, and netball. She loved to play soccer and joined the youth soccer team. Ripley also liked to go to the beach to swim.

GOING PRO

Ripley played for the Fulham United soccer club in Australia.

Ripley's parents took her to her first wrestling match when she was young. From that moment on, she was hooked! She watched wrestling matches whenever she could.

WWE wrestler The Miz **inspired** Ripley to become a **professional** wrestler. She started training as a teenager. She was the only woman in her training group. That did not stop her!

FAVORITES

FOOD
PIZZA

MUSIC GENRE
METAL

SPORTS TEAM
ADELAIDE FC

WRESTLER
THE MIZ

STILL DREAMING

When Ripley was 17, she tried out for WWE. Since the age to try out was 21, she was not able to join. She had to wait.

BECOMING BLOODY

TIMELINE

2013
Ripley joins RCW

2017
Ripley signs with WWE

Ripley made her wrestling **debut** in 2013. She started wrestling for Riot City Wrestling (RCW) in Australia. She went by her real name, Demi Bennett.

A few months later, Ripley wrestled Savannah Summers in the 2014 RCW Women's **Championship**. Ripley won! In 2016, she won the championship again.

2023

Ripley becomes the first woman to win Royal Rumble after beating 29 opponents

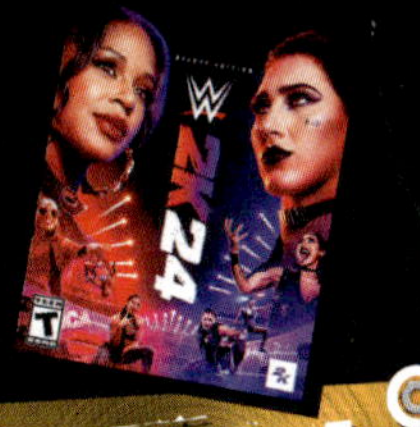

2024

Ripley becomes the cover star for the deluxe version of the video game *WWE 2K24*

Ripley continued to wrestle for **independent** companies across Australia. She moved from RCW to several other professional wrestling companies. She wrestled against women and men. The more she wrestled, the better she became.

Between 2015 and 2016, Ripley wrestled across Japan. She wrestled for many different Japanese wrestling companies.

In 2017, Ripley signed her first **contract** with WWE. She started using the name Rhea Ripley. She beat Miranda Alize in the first round of her very first match.

Ripley joined the WWE NXT **roster** in 2017. She defeated Toni Storm to become the first WWE NXT UK Women's Champion. Ripley was unstoppable!

TV DEBUT!

Ripley's first match on TV was the Mae Young Classic. It is an all-women's wrestling tournament.

TITLES

as of 2026

2x WWE WOMEN'S WORLD CHAMPION

1 NXT UK WOMEN'S CHAMPION

1 WWE RAW WOMEN'S CHAMPION

2x RCW WOMEN'S CHAMPION

1 NXT WOMEN'S CHAMPION

2x WWE WOMEN'S TAG TEAM CHAMPION

In 2021, Ripley formed a **tag team** with Nikki A.S.H. That year they won the women's tag team championship. In 2022, Ripley joined the dark **faction** called The Judgement Day.

In 2023, Ripley became the first woman to win a Royal Rumble match after beating 29 **opponents**. Later that year, she won the WrestleMania 39 Women's SmackDown Championship.

ROYAL RUMBLE 2023

NAME GAME

Ripley's nicknames, The Eradicator and The Nightmare, show opponents that she is tough. Her latest nickname is Rhea "Bloody" Ripley.

TOP MOVES

BIG BOOT

PUTS FOOT UP WHILE THE OPPONENT CHARGES FORWARD, DELIVERING A KICK TO THE FACE OR CHEST

RIPTIDE

PICKS UP THE OPPONENT FROM BEHIND AND SLAMS THEM TO THE MAT

PRISM TRAP

LIFTS THE OPPONENT UP WHILE HOLDING THEIR LOWER BACK AND LEGS

WHAT'S NEXT?

Ripley has climbed from independent companies to the top of WWE! She was even the cover star for the deluxe version of the video game *WWE 2K24*.

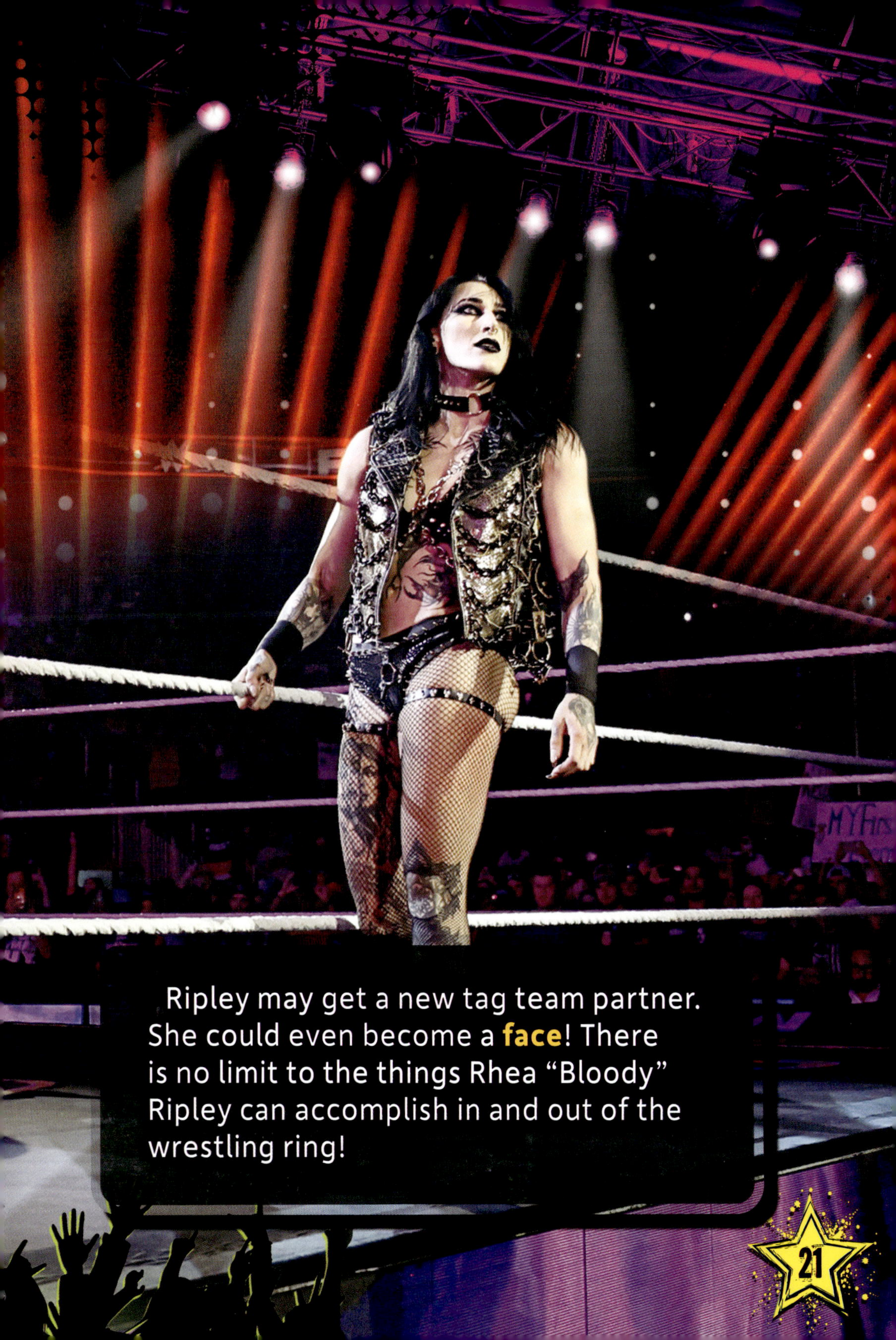

Ripley may get a new tag team partner. She could even become a **face**! There is no limit to the things Rhea "Bloody" Ripley can accomplish in and out of the wrestling ring!

GLOSSARY

championship—a contest to decide the best team or person

contract—an official agreement

debut—a person's first appearance or performance

face—a hero character

faction—a group of wrestlers who band together

heel—a villain character

independent—not controlled by a larger organization

inspired—gave someone an idea about what to do or create

match—a contest between two wrestlers

opponents—people that wrestle against one another

professional—related to a person or athlete who makes money wrestling

roster—a list of participants in wrestling

tag team—a pair or group of wrestlers who fight as a team

titles—championship statuses

World Wrestling Entertainment (WWE)—the world's largest professional wrestling and sports entertainment company

TO LEARN MORE

AT THE LIBRARY

Arnez, Lynda. *Be a Pro Wrestler.* Buffalo, N.Y.: Gareth Stevens Publishing, 2024.

Duling, Kaitlyn. *Bianca Belair.* Minneapolis, Minn.: Bellwether, 2027.

Leed, Percy. *Pro Wrestling Superstars.* Minneapolis, Minn.: Lerner Publications, 2025.

ON THE WEB

FACTSURFER

Factsurfer.com gives you a safe, fun way to find more information.

1. Go to www.factsurfer.com
2. Enter "Rhea Ripley" into the search box and click 🔍.
3. Select your book cover to see a list of related content.

INDEX

The images in this book are reproduced through the courtesy of: Sipa USA, front cover; Elsa/ Staff/ Getty Images, p. 3; Ronald Martinez/ Staff/ Getty Images, pp. 4, 5 (all); WWE/ Contributor/ Getty Images, pp. 6, 7, 8, 9, 11 (Rhea Ripley), 12, 14 (all), 15, 16, 18, 19 (all), 20, 21, 23; Zuma Press, Inc./ Alamy Stock Photo, pp. 10, 11 (The Miz); grey, p. 11 (pizza); Australia Football Logos/ Wikipedia, p. 11 (Adelaide FC); Alex Bierens de Haan/ Stringer/ Getty Images, p. 13 (2023); ZUMA Press Inc/ Getty Images, p. 18.